Ghost Radio

Other books by Dick Lourie

Anima (Hanging Loose)

4-Telling [With Robert Hershon, Emmett Jarrett, and Marge
Piercy] (The Crossing)

Letter to Answer (Unicorn)

Lies (Radical America)

Stumbling (The Crossing)

The Dream Telephone (The Crossing)

Ghost Radio

Dick Lourie

Hanging Loose Press
Brooklyn, New York

Acknowledgments

Some of these poems have appeared in the following journals: *ACM, Exquisite Corpse, Hanging Loose, The Massachusetts Review, MS, Noctiluca, Sun, Transfer,* and *Verse.*

"Forgiving Our Fathers" was first published in Dick Lourie's Hanging Loose Press collection *Anima.*

Hanging Loose Press wishes to thank the Literature Programs of the New York State Council on the Arts for a grant in support of this book's publication.

A portion of the author's royalties from this book are donated to the Delta Blues Museum and the Delta Blues Education Program in Clarksdale, Mississippi.

Library of Congress Cataloging-in-Publication Data

Lourie, Dick.

    Ghost radio / Dick Lourie.
      p. cm.
    ISBN 1-882413-49-0. -- ISBN 1-882413-48-2 (pbk.)
    I. Title.
    PS3562.083G48   1998
    811'.54--dc21   97-46107
                                      CIP

Cover art by Robin Tewes
Cover design by Caroline Drabik

Produced at The Print Center, Inc., 225 Varick St., New York, NY 10014, a non-profit facility for literary and arts-related publications. (212) 206-8465

For Denise

For John

Contents

Still Dancing

Ghost Radio

Believers in Synchronicity

The Little Richard Suite

1. the birth of Little Richard

on December 5th 1932
no one noticed an unusually bright
star glittering over Macon Georgia

it had been after all an eventful
year and astronomy was not the first
thing on their minds—height of the Depression
17,000 veterans march on
Washington   Roosevelt wins election
Hitler loses   though not by a landslide

so nobody sees this star settling right
above a house on Fifth Avenue: Bud
and Leva Mae's third child Ricardo Wayne
Penniman is born   just months after Cole
Porter's *Gay Divorcée* plays in New York
Hart Crane disappears at sea   Beecham founds
the London Philharmonic   and Johnny
Weissmuller makes his first Tarzan movie

believers in synchronicity nod
their heads here: but let's just remember that
our book of famous events doesn't list
the number of black folks lynched in Georgia
this year of our Lord 1932

2. succession

in Houston about 1953
Johnny Otis recalls hearing Richard
perform   he's already flamboyant (though
this is two years before the hits begin)

"I am the King of Rock and Roll" he says
"and also the Queen"   ah this is brilliant
the outrageous will always serve him well:
the clown act   the costumes the pompadour

"him?   that fool that queer   of course we don't see
him as a threat   he's a joke"   and of course
nothing was safe   their daughters   their sons   their
world—all changed   changed utterly as Yeats said

Richard in the forefront   Richard pounding
the piano of revolution that
would put an end to the America
I knew as a boy: where Norman Rockwell
—I recall seeing him perform—told us
"I am the King of your self-images
also the Queen"   but when we got through the
King was dead   long live King Little Richard

3. classic hits and oldies

so why do they call this "classic" I wondered
maybe they're trying to suggest the Athens
of Socrates and the "polis"   great drama
hubris and the start of this whole culture's
decline   soon to be followed by imperial Rome

well   I thought   that does make some kind of sense
out of the oddly named "classic hits" format
on my radio   from the Beatles through say
early Bruce: a greatness that carries just like
the Greeks the seeds of its own destruction

but if "classic hits" is like Athens what about
the "oldies" station next to it on the dial
the place for those of us who play in "all
fifties rock 'n' roll" bands   and whose love
begins with the Penguins and fades perhaps
with the very earliest Miracles

of course! I thought: "oldies" is the Heroic
Age   it's us Homer speaks of   in our wildness
camped before the walls of civilized Troy
eating   drinking   singing all night around our fires

this is not Athens with its endless gossip
about gods they only know from a distance
in our camp the gods make frequent visits
they bang our heads together to instruct us
they eat our food   jostling each other for
the best morsels and laughing among themselves

the gods say that sooner or later the city
will fall to us and they cheer us on   all night we
dance   and when we open our mouths the gods speak:
"a wop bob a loo mop a lop bam boom"

4. rock and roll   rhythm and blues

out on the iron range   1956
Bob Dylan was still Bobby Zimmerman
but (a biographer says) he listened
late at night when the radio could pick up the
distant stations that played black rhythm and blues

and when he sang like Little Richard in
the school talent show it was as if he
had landed on Mars   but since it was really
Minnesota   the Midwest   USA

what this means is that forty years later
I can be sitting back comfortably
in the poet's chair thinking about the past
while Little Richard preaches in church   gets
laughed at   hustled out of his royalties
and Dylan   though I love him still   is worth millions

BHS

as teenagers we lived in the fifties   and thought a great deal
about the smell of our own breath   we admired Karen the
cheerleader and wished we were like her   or else we were
in love with her secretly   and jealous of Tommy the half-
back who went out with her   then later even more jealous
of Bill the scholar who also went out with her   we ate lunch
in a dark wood booth every day thirty-eight years ago in the
luncheonette that isn't there anymore of course: too much
ketchup on the french fries   Buddy kept insisting   we
always ate there with the same few friends   who now have
disappeared into the rest of New Jersey

song embodying what I've learned in twenty-five years

in 1969 I was angry
at the usual suspects—President
Johnson-Nixon and the Republican-
Democrat party of money   power
corruption   and expensive dark suits

I saw the poor lying in the wreckage
of the Great Society   heads blown off
bodies mutilated   blood all over

they looked like Vietnamese   they looked like the
fifty-eight thousand Americans whose
lives we were trying to save with our hot
anger   we lost as you know   and I saw
the beast of capital as I viewed it
sucking us all up   shitting out our bones

what I've learned—so gradually it was
imperceptible until one day I
thought fifty-five years old and what have I learned—

is first that just my small stash of white middle-
class privilege has been more than enough
to purchase a life of reasonable
comfort—not in the belly of the beast but
say in some corner it hasn't yet noticed

and second that everything else is not
very much changed from 1969:
carefully I pick my way through the wreckage
to bring you this song for what it's worth

the gay issue in America

Patriotism and gay-bashing are the last refuge of the scoundrel.
—Mark Twain

let's get at the real issue here   it's not
"life style"   "special rights"   or "the homosexual
agenda"   it's genitals   and you have

taken a courageous stand on what you
believe   which is if I understand it
correctly that the penis belongs only
in the vagina or elsewhere on a
woman's body while the vagina may
touch a man anyplace but not a woman
is this a fair statement of your ideas?

and I take it you would enforce some rules:
penises must not touch one another
nor should my penis—assuming you and
I are both men—be in your mouth or your
anus and yours should not etcetera me

if we are women my vagina should not
touch yours nor should my hands lips knees or breasts
kissing might be a special case given
our culture's rituals of friendship but
certainly a man should not lick another
man's ear or neck or thigh   ditto women
does this reasonably sum up your views?

and if it's agreed that this is the real
issue can't we try to discuss our
differences sensibly?   before we
do why don't you go home tonight and just
keep repeating "your penis my vagina
my penis your vagina" and then take
one of each and call me in the morning

Delta blues tours

some people we met at the Clarksdale blues
festival said that as real Delta blues
fans they loved "X's" performance but that
"Y" seemed a bit too close to Piedmont style

and "Z" was flashy   much more like a soul
singer   mostly they preferred last year's show:
they don't understand that blues here is like
family   and that if we viewed things their way

we might love some old grandma blues but dis-
respect her son   maybe for his hair style
while his young cousins in their gold suits would
seem like complete strangers   Oh blues tourists!

come back next year without your definitons
and you will be welcomed with open arms and ribs

lyric sonnet

A book to come out soon is discussed in
my *Sunday Times*:   Yeats and Pound together
spending three winters at Stone Cottage on
the Sussex downs—the last in 1914

when modernism's in early blossom
war has broken out and the future lies
before them   while in New Orleans Buddy
Bolden's shadowy mantle waits for Armstrong

barely a teenager and Miles not yet born
my father is two years old in Brooklyn
his long uncertain life bound to color mine

and my own youth   a sacrament to the
trumpet and to poetry is far off
as love seems sometimes on dark afternoons

Jewish

if you're born a Jew you must stay a Jew
like being Irish Chinese Puerto Rican
Mohawk: you can move away   renounce your
birth but they'll always know you as a Jew

what's different is that no one can convert
to being Chinese while anybody
can become Jewish   this means that I as
a Jew have an identity I can't
change yet must share with anyone who asks

because it's hard to be attached to both
these facts with equal passion we tend to
grasp one or the other in shaping our
lives: those who are hotly fixed on their own
Jewish essence and whose fault is
arrogance   and those who can't forget that
everyone is potentially Jewish
and whose fault is sentimentality

when they speak the first says "there's no such thing as a
Palestinian"   the other says "the world is a Jew"

at the shore

for Abe Freedman and Isobel Rigg

where better than the Jersey shore to see
how everyone's perfect moments are so
different from everybody else's
even if we leave out the most private—
the two of us alone last night   full moon
slow dancing at the house by the lagoon

aside from that my own perfect moment is
a slow cruise right down the main boulevard
of Long Beach Island   that skinny sand spit
twenty miles long   not far from
Atlantic City—this is where I've come closest to

time travel: from the house my wife's parents
bought in the late fifties near the northern
tip   land of sand   scrub pines   and foxtail reeds
I can cruise slowly south to Beach Haven

where my parents used to rent each summer
where nothing lies between Barnegat Bay
and the great sea but miniature golf
and food joints with signs that still read "Custard"—
when I say "the shore" that's what I mean   and

now I pretend it's 1958—
lost between my junior and senior years
at Princeton I've stopped in to visit my
mother the social worker and my step-

father the lawyer   uncertain if I
should apply to medical school or if
there's anything else to do with my life

no one knows the future but in my car
cruising the island I pretend that I
do   and that it's 1958   and

that fifteen miles north my wife's a skinny
nine-year-old red haired kid who'd rather scrape
her dad's sailboat than dry dishes for her mom

perfect moment: thinking of my life I
smile cruising slowly in the sun down
Long Beach Boulevard   rhythm and blues on the
radio   I stop for a hot dog   I
drink coffee in my car   I cruise again
looking everywhere for just the right yard sale

George Bush and Peter Pan
(1991)

for Larry Duberstein

I may have figured out Bush's "thousand
points of light": that image from the '88
campaign for addressing problems (health care
crime   poverty   education)   with a
vast army of citizen volunteers

at the time I was puzzled—poets are
frequently unsure of whether something
is literal or metaphorical—

I thought first of Tinker Bell with her tiny
light dimming as Peter Pan begs children
who believe in fairies to clap their hands

until her spark grows bright again   looking
at Bush's points of light this way he is
urging us to "clap our hands"   meaning that

each of us should spend a few hours a week
in community service until schools
are better   the air is clean   our infant
mortality rate is down   and everyone's
got a place to live   a job   and day care

but recently I've wondered if his words
were really much less poetic: by this
vast "army of volunteers" did he mean
in fact the US armed forces? this makes

sense   then those "points of light " would be
the actual radiant flash and burn
of destruction from these weapons we were
wanting to try out   in that case yes George

you were both literal and clear and I
don't know why I should have been so puzzled

on the other hand when he said "solving
problems"   that may have been more in the line
of the figurative: "solving" then would
mean getting distracted by a small war

rather as if Peter Pan were to say
"never mind Tinker Bell for now—we
need all available volunteers to
go fight Captain Hook"   but then Peter Pan

took care of Tinker Bell before heading
off to face the enemy in single
combat: which would have been my choice for George
Bush and Saddam Hussein especially

since Bush seemed so personally concerned
about Kuwait   instead he made other
choices   no doubt with an eye to his re-
election   well   if I could clap my hands

together to prove that I believe in
poetic retribution and to wish
some appropriate fate for George Bush   I'd

say let him in his sleep tonight be struck
split open   flesh burned away by his own
thousand points of light: death and destruction
and of course here I am speaking meta-
phorically I think although I'm not sure

rest easy Bill Clinton

I got a note from one of my muses
saying he wanted to remind me I've
fallen behind in my now twenty-five-
year project of poems about our Presidents

I'm up to date on Bush as Peter Pan
Carter as good cop   Ford as fool   Nixon

as scum bag and Johnson as wounded steer
I haven't tagged Reagan yet but I think
I'd better move right along to Clinton—
even this early things are only too clear

question: has Bill Clinton betrayed the left?
this depends on what you were expecting:
would you say Pat Boone betrayed rock and roll?
over the last forty years have the giant
TV networks betrayed our culture's humane values?
has Arnold Schwarzenegger betrayed the
great tradition of Shakespearean acting?

Bill Clinton? you were expecting maybe
George McGovern? Ron Dellums? Tom Harkin?

this was the first election I recall
where a moderate Republican disguised
as a Democrat ran against a shit head
disguised as a moderate Republican

rest easy Bill Clinton: when my complete
Presidential Poems are published I
will not accuse you of betraying the left

Ronald Reagan: night shift

right after he announced that it was now
morning in America Reagan appeared
to fall asleep for eight years   Ron van Winkle
snoozing at Cabinet meetings   catching
a nap it was clear wherever he could

newly released documents however show
that all this time he was really working the
night shift so of course most days he'd nod off

late nights Reagan   brilliant   sharp   alert   would
sit in the private screening room and watch
old movies   he and the White House projectionist
the only ones awake   film spooling in the dark
Reagan coolly analyzing   creating
policy based on these realities

all of John Wayne's films of course   and his own
(providing a kind of general approach
to looking at problems and solutions)
and many other instructive classics

was it by chance the rich just got richer
the poor homeless?   no it was his response
to *The Scarlet Pimpernel*   Central
America policy?   Carmen Miranda
the great strides in civil rights?   some long nights
spent poring over *Birth of a Nation*

before meetings with leaders of the
Soviet Evil Empire sometimes he'd invite
his closest advisors to join him for
a double feature: *FBI Story*
and *Flash Gordon Meets Ming the Merciless*

in my mind I see them—Ron and his top guys
huddled in the screening room—as the
burlesque outlaws in my favorite scene from
Blazing Saddles sitting around the flickering
campfire asking each other to please pass the beans

control

suddenly one day things got turned around
so that all birth control devices were
objects that men had to put into their bodies:
the most widely used were the pills that might
give you headaches and occasionally

cancer   the others were less convenient
but appeared to have with some exceptions
a generally higher level of
safety: ingenious machinery — caps
and valves   tubing   springs   pumps — all sturdily
constructed of plastic, metal, and glass

we found it difficult to get used to
inserting these things into our own selves
and feeling them there   we envied the
freedom of the women and hoped they would
sympathize with us

spring

"the Morris dancers are at it again"
I said to my wife who was stretched out on
the couch in her attractive black tights and
the sky-blue sweater (color of her eyes)

reading the *Boston Globe* in which looking
over her shoulder I saw the headline
about the Rhode Island guys up at dawn
yesterday to celebrate the first day
of spring in the customary fashion

of Morris dancers while she and I marked
the same occasion with a long slow walk
on the beach at Rockport where we had first
decided almost fifteen years ago

to get married   "ah synchronicity!"
I thought   heading upstairs to my desk a
glass of red wine an empty notebook page

because I had suddenly recognized
my remark about the dancers as an
exact ten-syllable line   the line I
have been using for just now thirty years

since my friend Mitch suggested I try it
and out came my first syllabic poem:
sad young man on a New York City beach—

that *was* long ago and some years before
I met my wife and began seeing how
essential it is to celebrate spring

the sacramental life

when my wife and I dine by candlelight
smile   click our wine glasses together I
feel both romance and intimacy   so

when a friend says he loves intimacy
but isn't romantic I'm surprised that
they're separable: to me romance is
just like communion: eat this meal   drink this
wine   the only path to intimacy

and before this marriage I kept trying
the same thing—which like a false miracle
would last maybe through breakfast then dissolve—
I always blamed my fellow congregants

but if my friend's right I should not have been
complaining: what's wrong with romance for an
evening   and unlike intimacy
it's never hard to find some new convert
for a quick Mass   as for me and my wife

it may not be transubstantiation
after all   but just two things hitting at
once—more like synchronicity: here's the
wine and here's the sink where we'll wash the wine
glasses tomorrow   here's the candle   let's
carry it upstairs   here's her face in the
shadowy light and here's the bed we've been
waking up in for several thousand mornings

team sports

when the 1995 World Series
pitted "Braves" against "Indians" the great
excitement of Native Americans

at the kind of respect they were getting
through nationwide TV images of
their cultures—big chiefs   feathers   tomahawks—
soon led other ethnic groups to wonder
if they should be expecting the same   and

sure enough within a few more seasons
the Washington Greasy Guinea-Wops faced
the Green Bay Kikes with their mascot "Jew Boy"

who does the comic Yiddish accent wrapped
in a green and gold prayer shawl which he dips

into the Gatorade for laughs   wailing
"Oy veh ist mir" after every touchdown

blues from Clarksdale

for Big Jack Johnson and the Oilers

after driving all day from New York to
a bar the size of two small living rooms
in a college town the size of two small
bars   they start unpacking the van: by nine

Chet's at the drums with his Guinness   David's
guitar shifts into swing   Hooter flatpicks
his bass   and when Chet asks the crowd "are you
ready for star time?"   and when the crowd parts for

Jack   who comes up   lifts a guitar   plays—it
seems to you that he could have walked here from
Clarksdale   through hard juke joints along dark roads
not honored enough beyond the Delta

and when he starts to sing you wonder how
many hundreds of years he's been traveling

Cleaning the Desk

cleaning the desk

before I came home from the hospital
I had started planning to clean my desk—
two days after surgery dozing on
morphine I opened my eyes and wondered
how many stackable plastic letter
trays I had at home and what would be the
most practical categories for sorting
the dusty piles of mail that lay everywhere

last time I cleaned up it was a different desk
I took all the stuff off the old door balanced
on the two filing cabinets so that
Larry could build my elegant new desk:
fifty-third birthday present to myself

I also cleaned my desk when I was
forty-two   Abby and I getting married
and I lugged everything to Boston from
Ithaca where actually I had
two desks   big ones   though I don't remember why

before that I'd had no desk for several
years—so many apartments   Peekskill   New Paltz
and that tiny house where Virginia and I
tried to be happy   no room for desks there

in the mid-sixties   cheap East Village pads
I distinctly recall just using the
kitchen table for everything   of course
I cleaned my desk thoroughly when I left
college though the one at home in New Jersey
I had used all through high school just kept on
accumulating papers—I should ask
my mother whatever happened to that one

and I had a little blue desk when I
was eight but I believe it was the kind where
everything got stuffed underneath the hinged
desk top so it never needed cleaning

the question is (when you're trying to plan
something as I was   lying there relaxed
and thoughtful)   whether you'd be better off
reviewing the history a little—
how did you get your desks clean in the past?
why did that first marriage fail?—or just looking
ahead: suppose I have say fourteen letter trays
will they make one big stack without falling down

1954

for Bob Greenberg

to understand everything you have to
imagine 1954 when our
idea of a hot time with music
was the nine-piece approximation of
"big bands" that performed for Tuesday assemblies
at the high school in Bogota New Jersey

we played our tattered arrangements of *Stardust*
String of Pearls   In the Mood   compelled to re-
study the ancient texts in the face of
what popular music had turned into:
1954's big hits were *Ebb Tide*
Baubles Bangles and Beads   I Love Paris
and *How Much is that Doggie in the Window*

teenagers playing our parents' music
we were content—it had some excitement
maybe like old movies   and it was not
I Believe or *Stranger in Paradise*

now do you see how *Earth Angel* seized us:
the shock of waking after a long sleep
this was the year we all fell in love at once
listening to the Penguins in Judy
Horton's basement and never went back to
Glenn Miller   we danced closer in Judy's
basement where the Drifters and the Harptones

waited for us and we knew they would
at last separate us from our parents
who might or might not respect black people
but certainly wouldn't listen to their music

it wasn't just that we were sixteen in
1954—the year broke open
behind us as we passed   our lives split in
two by rock and roll which was our future

rage

this is when I'm glad I don't have a child
these times when I spill soup on the floor then
feel like kicking the cat hard because I'm
angry at myself   or when I open

the cellar door and the cat dashes down
the stairs   I know it's because cats like cellars
but the flower of rage suddenly blooms
in my head   my anger at her for dis-
pleasing me is the sour and strong fragrance:
I am high on it immediately—

bones and muscles charged I run after her
down the stairs   through the dark spaces among
the cartons and tools yelling   "get out of here
I'll kill you   I'm not satisfied" and I
perceive the cat as insolent   "you knew
that I did not want you to come down here"

I am screaming at the cat now until she's
cornered   her back to the stairs   she turns and
runs up out of the cellar   I'm left
shaken and hurt in the cool darkness

as if someone had seized hold of that red
blossom and was trying once and for all
to pull it out by the roots

an address on Greek myth given during a short visit to Ithaca New York

good evening   this is my first visit
in twelve years so I've been somewhat nervous
thanks for being here: Ithaca's the place
where I have most often fallen in love
maybe it's my fate   or some genetic

predisposition—since my parents met
here as college students—and just like their
marriage all my Ithaca loves ended
badly   for them: passion   a child   confused
betrayal   divorce   and now
fifty years with me as a memento

in my case it was more like having my
heart ripped out by eagles every few months
and still—walking down your pleasant streets—I
can hear those cries   so for me visiting

isn't a climactic event as when
Odysseus finally comes home   it's the
middle of the story: his journey to
Hell where he converses with his mother's ghost

baggage

when I think of myself in my mother's
body I imagine some kind of bag
with me inside it   when my friends tease me
it's often about my suitcases   brief-
cases   shopping bags   shoulder bags   gym bags
milk crates   back packs   and instrument cases

I'm the man of a thousand containers
born from the child with his baggage always
packed to travel between divorced parents
famous for my car's back seat   my basement

my study   the clutter I try to stuff
everywhere so I can just have it
with me and not be forced to choose what of
my past it might be safe to throw away

stop me before I pack my things again:
bringing them out to the car each morning
on safari to the office   keep me
from showing up at band rehearsal with
my luggage carrier   tape recorder
wireless mike and attachments   extra long
cables   spare amplifier just in case—
they tell me I'm only the sax player
why do I have more stuff than ten drummers

and why do short weekend trips resemble
diasporas   vast tribal migrations   why
indeed   or as Doctor Kriegsfeld great wise-
ass of therapists used to say "who should
we ask?"   how do you expect me to choose
which parent to keep   what things I *won't* need
on my next trip?   I can't do that—any
more than I could decide to just throw it
all away and climb back into the bag

connections

no phone: and I don't mean on purpose or
not yet (as when you have just moved) but un-
expectedly: one Friday late afternoon
in this town you've come hundreds of miles to
for a temporary job   all your friends
elsewhere and naturally you did get
the phone hooked up right away

but now just a week later the "Business
Office" as it's called has had you shut off
for some reason and the "Repair Service"
insists nothing can be done without further
authorization which can't happen till Monday

of course I don't mean *you*—I just say that
to pretend everyone's like me   it is
me angry and frightened   my connection
to my friends snapped: I drive to a phone booth and call
them all just to make sure they know they will
not be able to reach me this weekend if they need to

while I'm out I have something to eat then
buy food for later at the apartment
don't you always feel more secure when you're
eating? I'm sorry I mean me again
by the time I get back though
I remember there were some people I
tried to reach before who weren't home and
I could use some ice cream too so I make

another trip out and back: now I think
the activity and the food have calmed me
down enough to sleep   I pick up the phone
one more time just in case it works   it doesn't of course

but couldn't it somehow get fixed despite what they said?
couldn't it ring after I have fallen
asleep—I'd stumble over to it half
glad half scared and it would be myself

in fifth grade the little fat boy just moved
into a new town mother remarried
who eats to feel better and clowns to make friends but
seems earnest now with something shaky in his voice
saying "you're the only one I can talk to"

my father's wire recorder

I remember it as the late forties
the wire unwound horizontally from
one spool to another   like the reels of
the tape recorder soon to drive it off
the market—the wire seemed always to go
wrong somewhere   maybe in rewinding—and
to end up in a tangle on the floor

even where it got straightened out the sound
quality was poor   but I remember
my father's excitement—through a long life
he's been enamored of gadgets   if they
don't work right they can simply be replaced:

the wire recorder by the reel-to-reel
tape   then cassettes   he always wanted to
record family events   I am his
oldest child   after he and my mother
got divorced he remarried   had four more
that was when he got the wire recorder

he couldn't really answer when I asked
why they had gotten divorced—he had none
of my mother's bitterness   instead he
was vague   "sometimes people just aren't comfortable
together"   I pictured him with the wire
recorder   when it stopped working he got
something else that served the same function and

he was perfectly happy   except he could
never bring himself to throw things away
somewhere in his basement: the tangled wires

fortieth high school reunion

right away I know why I've skipped all the
others: fear of meeting my seventeen-
year-old pudgy honor student self   a
nice kid with professional prospects who

walks right up to me now while at the bar
Bob chats with Lorraine   Gil shows Fred snapshots
from his vacation   "hello son" I say   though
I've never had kids   don't think of him as

my son   I'm just scared he won't approve of
me—I know he's looking forward to a
life of order   neatness   as a doctor
lawyer   husband   father   not a man with

desks full of unread mail   too little sleep
chaos and dirt in all the odd corners
in fact he looks right through me—a good job
of pretending that I'm not here at all

commemoration

1994 marks the fiftieth
anniversary of my parents' divorce
they plan to celebrate it separately

my mother has stopped taking piano
lessons   tired she says of feeling "pressure"
she'll still play Bach and Mozart and Chopin
but won't need to prepare an assignment
for the teacher like a kid in school

retired to the small world of her house she
looks back on forty good years in her view
with my stepfather and sees the time since
his death as her time to start growing old
peacefully: this fiftieth anniversary year
she won't think at all about my father
except possibly when she looks at me

my father is very pleased when I call
I'm the oldest   the only child of his
first marriage   but he lives in the present

knowing there's something that sets me apart
from the others but not always sure of
what it is   he had thirty good years with
my stepmother who died too young   then he

stayed lonely with a succession of women
he wanted to keep him from loneliness
now he's married again at eighty-one
this year my mother will not cross his mind
at all and I'm afraid to ask him what
it is that he remembers about her

Ebbets Field

because I decided not to have sons
or daughters certain doors closed while others
keep falling open behind me though I've
tried to force them shut: like the gate into

Ebbets Field where as a child I saw the
Dodgers play—whatever it is that broke
between me and my father stands holding
that portal wide   beyond it when I

turn to look is the unattainable
sweet green that makes me cry   so I try not
to look but up ahead the doors are closed

and on the radio Peewee Reese's
son is describing their annual trip
to the Hall of Fame celebration where

they share a hotel room lying in the
dark while cool mist rolls in off Lake Glimmerglass

the persistence of memory

my father's confused at eighty-four—from
what my sister says on the phone he sounds
worse than when I visited in March—he's lost
track even more of what to call things   the
names of people in his photo albums

"but the one person he never forgets"
she tells me "is you"   me   the oldest   does
long-term memory hang on more? they looked
at photos together last weekend   me
as an infant in the bathtub   "look" my
father said "there's Dick"   "yes" my sister said

after she told me last night I dreamed this:
we are all at the old house we went to
every summer   I'm eighteen   my brother and
sisters are kids   everyone's on that porch

facing the mountains   a crowd of people
has joined us   I see friends from my present
life   relatives who died before I was
born   my wife   even my mother   though it's
the house my father bought years after their

divorce   we are all sitting down now to
lunch   here's Betty the stepmother I love
who will die before I realize how
much   she's bringing iced tea from the kitchen

we are all happy eating sandwiches:
for some reason my father is missing
he's just not here and I can't remember his name

forgiving our fathers

for M.K.

maybe in a dream: he's in your power
you twist his arm but you're not sure it was
he that stole your money   you feel calmer
and you decide to let him go free

or he's the one (as in a dream of mine)
I must pull from the water but I never
knew it or wouldn't have done it until
I saw the street-theater play so close up
I was moved to actions I'd never before taken

maybe for leaving us too often or
forever when we were little   maybe
for scaring us with unexpected rage
or making us nervous because there seemed
never to be any rage there at all

for marrying or not marrying our mothers
for divorcing or not divorcing our mothers
and shall we forgive them for their excesses
of warmth or coldness   shall we forgive them

for pushing or leaning for shutting doors
for speaking only through layers of cloth
or never speaking or never being silent

in our age or in theirs or in their deaths
saying it to them or not saying it—
if we forgive our fathers what is left

giving up coffee

I swear it was an accident   I just
needed abdominal surgery: no
food or drink for twenty days   incision
like a long zipper fly   many hours
soothed by morphine   and I'd had no coffee

in our family you nursed the baby then
gave it a small sip of café au lait
you weaned it onto black coffee and there
it stayed   this was my life my elixir

in high school we were the diner generation
burger? sure   fries? maybe   coffee? always
at college how else could you stay awake
all night finishing a term paper

then I was a beatnik   the coffeehouse
my academy and my temple   I
never liked bars   double espresso please!

and in my poems over thirty years
references to sex or love: ninety-five
politics: one hundred forty-seven
death: two hundred twelve   coffee: six thousand

I was highly evolved: fresh roasted beans
grinder   gold filter   glass-lined white carafe
now what?   when I'm tired I sleep   and when I'm
awake I focus   I agree my mind's more clear

so shall I now embrace this change like a
new and steady marriage   or just go back
to the old romances that lift me so high
only to break my heart until the next cup

news to me

I'm surprised to learn that in all these years
since first being discovered the inner
child seems not to have grown up yet—and he's
quite open about it when I ask why:

"not my job" he says "to grow up—even
though (now that I've showed you how) you can weep
for the past yourself   someone's still got to
be responsible for the murderous
rage department"   now I'm really surprised

"you?   I've always thought of these urges to
insult strangers   to kill those I love most
as the work of my grown-up self at its
most twisted   the monster I have tried to
avoid   not you the child I've struggled so
long to reach"   "dumb fuck" the inner child screams
in my ear   "asshole   you're too stupid to live"

at fifty-nine

was it Keats or Shelley who liked that word
"forlorn"?   my choice would be "loose-leaf"   how it
suggests a small neat animal slipping
through the brush in a manicured forest

how it calls up my fat adolescence
when nothing fit or seemed in place except
the notebooks I took to school   not those cheap
spirals   wire unstitching to stab your thumb

but real three-hole notebooks   and dividers
with polished windows—amber/green/red/clear/
blue—so in school at least things were under
control   all the subjects neatly labeled

a dream: my life as loose-leaf   amber/laugh
green/write   red/play sax   clear/love wife   blue/fear death

Still Dancing

pastoral

"nothing has changed!" my wife's brother Jeffrey
shouts when I put *A Girl Has to Know* by
the G-Clefs onto my old turntable

A girl has to know that she's wanted
"come on Tess!" he says to his wife   "want to
dance?"   and right there in our house they start to
slow dance across the ratty Persian rug

I think to myself: what? nothing has changed?
when this song came out   1962
they were both in high school   now they've got two
kids and they've come to Boston to visit
the one in college who builds computers

A girl has to know that she's needed
not to mention that the G-Clefs picture—
full color on the front page of today's
Boston Herald Sunday magazine—shows
five guys on the far side of fifty in
white tuxes   not teenagers in string ties

A girl has to know that you love her
perhaps something has snapped in Jeffrey's head
(and I notice Tess did not turn him down)
maybe hearing the song just connected
a few stray synapses in both of them

so in their minds they know what year it is
now but their next point of reference back
is those early sixties: they're like the guy
in the Grace Paley story who loses
twenty years from a stroke and becomes a
sweeter person—of course this moment will
pass but meanwhile I see that they're still dancing

high school in the fifties

for us   then   high school was not only
a building   or a process   it was a name
for the culture we lived in which was
felt like an atmosphere: it was the place
the condition you stayed in until you could
get to college where eventually
life as a grown-up would come to collect you

but what everyone now calls "the fifties"
that wasn't us: that was the hoods with their
polished cars   and it was the girls who we
knew were not going to get to college

and what all this nostalgia now is for—
the haircuts and the jackets   the night-time
cruising like happy and dangerous fish—
that present moment was always theirs   like
the prisoner's free choice of that great last meal

and there was almost an understanding
between them and us   they owned the present
as we did the future   they tolerated
our intellect because we didn't insist
on taking over   we were there but silent:
a thoughtful audience

and although sometimes they scared us   these people—
their bright clothes and their gaze of such hunger
nail polish   the sudden fist fights   and their
actual practice of sex—still we should have been
more scared for them: should have seen their space closing
in on them as ours opened out   and we should have known

that they would be the working class   that they would be
trapped in babies and the most punishing jobs
just when we were being freed into college
where we expected to begin taking up our
inheritance of social and political power

and now I wish I could find them all again
these hoods   these bright girls of my youth
I'd say   "look   it's me   I think now finally
I can talk to you and I really want
to let you know what I have found out about
all that stuff I set out to inherit
then maybe we could all pile into your
car and go cruising tonight and look for
something to do."

poem for my uncle Sam Scheiner's 65th birthday, November, 1989

I

not long ago when Leadbelly played *The Midnight Special* you were sitting at his feet: a teenage socialist singing and

learning to call square dances   listening to the Almanac Singers   Pete Seeger Woody Guthrie   at parties in New York the Second World War around the corner

and it seems quite recent that you were an artist marrying my Aunt Gloria a father in Brooklyn then a social worker (some would prefer the term "trouble

maker") directing Philadelphia's loudest Senior Citizens Center whose difficult members simply refused to do as they were told   insisting on what they called their democratic process—just one more product of your social work Sam

II

but could you have been so young such a short time ago   so it appears   since what we have come to expect of age is that it should bestow a certain softening of anger   a kind of mellowing we've learned to call "maturity"   while in you

the struggle instead burns on as if you
didn't know that one is supposed to grow
less angry about the world   as if right
in the next room the Almanacs might be
working on a new song about George Bush
that they'll be asking you to introduce

as if we were all still in Brooklyn on
a Saturday night where the young left is
ready to square dance and later to start
organizing the next demonstration

and at family parties when you sit
around with your children   nieces   nephews
singing *The Midnight Special* no one's voice
Sam Scheiner   is louder than yours

justice

It's been reported that when the Beatles
were introduced to Steve Cropper   white genius
of black Memphis music   the four of them
all stood as one and bowed from the waist: an

appropriate homage I'd say   displaying their
good sense and making one wish that those who buy
records were that astute   instead   as we know
Steve Cropper's name is not yet a household word

except when compared with that of Lowman Pauling
his own acknowledged inspiration   now
forgotten   who all through the forties and
fifties played guitar and sang with the Five Royales

black musicians making black people's music
in the USA of lynchings and Jim
Crow   colored water fountains and early
death for Negroes who didn't know their place.

In a better world we would all stand up
you and I   John   Paul   George   Ringo   and Steve
"The Five Royales" we'd say   as if we were
on a stage   proudly introducing them
before a huge enthusiastic crowd

"Johnny Tanner and Eugene Tanner on
lead vocals" we'd say   "Jimmy Moore   Otto Jeffries and
Obediah Carter singing harmony
and on bass harmony and guitar
Lowman Pauling   Ladies and Gentlemen" we'd say

"this is like gospel sweetness caught and
held to earth by the sting of that guitar—
soul starts here"   we'd say   "and doo wop starts here
so will you please welcome the Five Royales"
and then we would all kneel and kiss their shiny shoes

first love poem in a long time

loving a woman not as your mother
but really different from that is so
difficult: you go to the beach together
there's plenty of sand all right and warm sun
but the breeze is cool   you kiss but it's not like
that time on the beach with _____ when the Kiss on the Beach
just by itself made everything else go away
or stop while the afternoon lingered for days

this time it's like a kiss and seems to remain
firmly in context: you can tell just how
long it takes   you never lose touch with the blue
towel you're sitting on   and instead of
being engulfed you keep feeling lips
bodies   both of you distinct   there all the time

and the water is so cold you think first
of your heart   "could it just stop from the shock
if I go in past my ankles?"   but to your
embarrassment she's already been in
once today   so although she's nice enough
not to brag or insist you decide to try it

but now she's drying off so you go alone
not like those days with _____ when you felt like
twins or halves of the same body   that comfort
of companionship everywhere   every
moment   today your heart keeps on but un-
accompanied as you grab a breath and plunge
into a wave   the ocean just as cold
as you thought   what a strange day this has turned out —

61

absolutely certain together but
also entirely separable
as if each of you could leave and return
without loss   your heart of course has not stopped
from the cold   you even feel good going to
dry off   nothing at all like those old times with
some other some shadowy but completely
absorbing person   when you bathed in the warm
sea   wishing only to stay there   never come out

the tenor sax and the Brooklyn Dodgers

to me the music's more important than
my instrument   let me have r&b
soul   blues   I'd give up the sax   learn guitar
anything so I could play what I love

but I know others whose passion for flute
violin   trumpet   would make them beg you
for any kind of music: just let them
play it on the instruments they cherish—
so different from my way of seeing things

though it's true I did look at baseball that
way: when the Dodgers—instrument of my
passion—left Brooklyn I lost all of my
interest in the game—so I can't say
my approach to life has been consistent

as for love I viewed it more like music
than baseball: knowing exactly what I
wanted to hear and switching instruments
whenever they weren't producing the
right sound which of course was just in my head

after all those years playing out of tune
what I needed instead was the Dodgers
and finding you was like walking into
Ebbets Field   love is baseball to me now
always getting it right doesn't matter
so long as I don't have to give you up
and I love you my sweet Campanella

twelve-bar blues

each verse of the blues tells a story in
three parts: a proposition is made then
repeated and then we're told its outcome

or you could say each verse tells a story
about birth: father   mother   and then child
told over and over very slowly

one

we start to play   someone sings a line   maybe
"Bach and Basie used to be my thing"   what
do you mean father?   but he won't answer
we have to wait for our mother to speak

two

"let me tell you people"   the verse goes on
"Bach and Basie used to be my thing"   we're
more anxious now   mother   please explain but
it's too late the child is coming soon and

three

so the singer moans "but since that woman
left me all I listen to is BB King"
the story's told the child is delivered
but suddenly what should be the final
chord is taking us to another verse

repeat

the music has brought us around again
to the next retelling   we are so tired
always trying to get it right but each
time the child seems to slip away: we're afraid
of losing it   we keep on playing till
we're exhausted and they turn out the lights

the singer leaves the stage   we put away
our instruments   happy we tried and sad
that we failed but how close we came this time
to finding a home for that blues child so
far out there drifting and drifting on the blue night waves

Blues lyric from Jimmy Lewis: *How Long is a Heartache Supposed to Last*
Last line paraphrased from Charles Brown: *Drifting*

doo wop

after the Ink Spots and the Mills Brothers
after the Golden Gate Quartet and the
gospel choirs   suddenly—or so it seemed—
something else was born as the forties closed

it was the music but also the names—
like the Ravens   Orioles   Dominoes
like the Clovers   the Five Keys   the Drifters—
that were new   and then the syllables came

the Crows sang "dit dit duh dit dit"   the Chords
answered "Sh' Boom"   the Penguins cried "wah oo"
and the Five Satins said "shoo dooten shooby doo"
passwords to the secret of doo wop harmony:

that as you sing through the same set of chords
song after song only one or two notes
at a time have to change and that if yours
is wrong you're never far from one that fits

this is the music of empowerment
not for what it says but for how it's made
all you need is four people and a place to
meet   it's the music of teenage romance
that still moves me at fifty-five   gray hairs
and all   it's the Jackie Robinson of
pop music breaking the color line forever

and it's something you can't do by yourself
if the blues is a solitary child
slowly drifting away while we try to
rescue it   doo wop is a few friends on
the corner who all speak at once as a sign that
their voices shall be inseparable

life and art

they tell me that as husband and father
you display many fine qualities not
apparent in a roommate   surprising?   no

after all   when we shared that house for five
years we were young (at least when we started)
and our life together then encouraged

specialization for survival   not
growth and development: you cooked I washed
I picked the towels up off the bathroom floor
you fixed the furnace and the cars   when we
quarreled I wouldn't listen you wouldn't
respond   is that what's called adaptation?

a joke: you said we were the Odd Couple
Felix and Oscar   that artfully matched
pair   the compulsive and the slob   only
you'd never say who was which: clearly you
wanted me to be both and you neither

in our most famous argument you claimed
that in person I'd turned out not to have
the clarity and strength of my poems
you felt this to be a kind of cheating

but then I'd made the same mistake: loving
your music so much I thought your life too
must have that balance—word and act   voice and
mandolin—twenty years later I start
realizing I should pay attention

to the instrument not the lyrics: some
kindness you perform while I'm still straining
to decipher what it is you've been mumbling

friends who knew us both said as we entered
rock and roll together *"you* are playing
in a band with *Howie?"*   but it has worked

suggesting no answers to me on life
and art—only that they remain enmeshed
and that as the ancestors used to remark "you
are a stranger but you're a friend of mine"

Song lyrics are from the Carter Family's *Hello Stranger.*

theories of alien abduction: poem for my mother's 80th birthday

like everyone else I could easily
be convinced that I was kidnapped at birth
put to sleep for ten years   taken to this
planet and raised by kind strangers starting
about age eleven   this idea

would have explained my mystification
at twenty-five—I have no resemblance
to these people I have called my parents
maybe these dream-like childhood memories
were implanted when I was brought here from
my far-off home—at thirty-five I was
certain of it   since then I've grown less sure

until in my fifties I look closely
at my mother who seems almost familiar:
isn't this my own deep need for music?
don't I recognize these geologic
forces clashing far below her surface?
can this anxiety about checking
the gas on the stove and locking the front
door be coincidence?   or the gift for
easy talking   the capacity for
devotion?   so I'm about ready to

acknowledge her as my source: welcome
mother   to your eighty-first year: I should
live so long and in such spirits   at last

I am compelled to abandon all my
theories about alien abduction
concluding that I am Doris's child
and I alone am left to know what this means

Apollo

for Chris, Ilanga, Payme, Ray, and Teddy

my cousin the young drummer and his band
have that capacity of youth to change
endlessly provocatively and at
a terrific pace—when I first saw them
they were all black leather and torn t-shirts
their music   "speed metal"   was like having
a heart attack during a gun battle

when I saw them again they had a horn
section   two lead singers   they wore lots of
plaid and suspenders   they danced across the
stage   the music had more layers   hip hop
grunge   how many identities had they
passed through in just these few years of living?

the musicians I play with are older
and everything seems just the opposite:
their identity   steady as mountains
remains   it's the years of living that pass by
even me   more than ten years now as a
sax player and I have no urge to change
my ways   I want to play the blues   I want
to sink into r&b and soul and
stay there forever   long live rock and roll

and I think of the Perfect Blend in their
white suits on stage stepping   their hearts aflame
with Motown harmony   their day to day
jobs didn't matter one left town some kind
of trouble—he's back   one's in jail   he'll be
out soon   have years and years passed?   it doesn't
matter   they talk about starting again

and the G-Clefs   who are my age   oh shit
no one's my age!   who played the Apollo
as teenage singing sensations younger
than my cousin   and have not forgotten
how to do it   their voices shift and match—
each identity so sure that they look
like they're exactly together even
when they are dancing in five directions

what shall we say about their steadiness?
nothing   we will just go to hear them sing
music intact through more than forty years
and as we age into wherever we're
heading we ask your blessing Apollo

another road less traveled by

For JM

most tenor sax players boogied along
together   with friendly competitions
among themselves and the different styles
until the late forties when they pulled up

to the great crossroads where   like Frost   each one
had to choose: down this path a hard life in jazz
but respect from colleagues and devotion
from listeners who would grow old with you

the other led to rock and roll: flat on
your back in a sharp suit honking for teens
who loved you till those guitars seduced them—
and from your jazz brothers: cold scorn   so let's

not forget as we kneel before Coltrane to lie
down and kick our feet up for Big Jay McNeely

comparative linguistics

Steve Allen had a smug routine for making
fun of rock and roll: he'd pretend he was
reading aloud something he thought profound
he'd peer into the camera   recite
with exaggerated refinement some
"shoo-doot" or "dom-be-dooby-dom" refrain

pausing for feeling and emphasis   the
point being what fools we were to believe
the wordless syllables could carry such
significance   but the joke was on Steve

who—smart guy though he was—must have seen the
world in terms of the "civilized" and the
"primitive" separated by language
as if words were highly reliable
conveyances for feeling and meaning
and rock and roll syllables were useless

but forty years later—in my soul at
least—Steve Allen is a small carping voice
tiny blurred face on an old TV set
language coming out of his mouth facile
signifying nothing   while rock and roll

still glows with history and passion when
somebody goes Ka-Ding-Dong-Ding-Dong-Ding

love note

since you'll have left for your meeting before
I get home   don't forget to throw all your
laundry into the basket: I'll take it
downstairs   sort things into light and dark loads

and wash them all   I'll put your jeans in the
dryer and hang up the turquoise plaid shirt:
pledging I would keep you in clean clothes was
as serious as all the other vows

how much underwear have I laundered   how
many of your little socks have I chased
back into pairs for you—this might make a
better song than "How Deep Is the Ocean"

at the formal dinner I admire your new
dress but what I love is your clean white handkerchief

questions about the blues

"shall we go out and hear some music?" I
say to my wife   "there's a blues band tonight
at Johnny D's"   to which her unfailing
reply is "a black band or a white band?"

this is the wrong question of course but not
that far wrong—my wife as a student at
the University of Chicago
went to the South Side clubs   heard Magic Sam
Junior Wells   Muddy Waters in their prime

and I could say "what about the others
Charlie Musselwhite   Elvin Bishop   the
white exceptions?"   but that just proves the rule

her question's wrong because the point's not "if
they're black they re probably good musicians"
or "they invented blues so they hold the
copyright" but I'm not sure there is a
right question   and in any case my wife

is entitled to her own precautions:
she's like someone with a taste for great wine
and just so I won't waste her evening
she wants to know if I'm offering her
a bottle of Sneaky Pete in a paper bag

The Perfect Blend

for Garrison, Kenny, EJ, and Charles

I   at the Sky Cap

from the crowd's response you would think it was
the Temptations when the house lights go out
in 1986 at the Sky Cap
Plaza on Warren Street in Roxbury

and when the spotlight finds EJ   Kenny
Garrison   and Charles in sparkling blue suits
poised at the back of the central aisle in
the rented function hall   they do look like

they might be on their way to Motown-style
success   these are not the Temptations though
or the Tops   it's the Perfect Blend   four guys
black   trying to keep it together in Boston

then the band on stage starts up   the singers
walk   dance down the aisle   the people at the
tables on either side go wild with love

I am the sax player in this band and
besides our guitarist probably the
only person not black in the whole room

do I feel like an anthropologist?
no   more like a guest in somebody's house
glad to be here   lucky to have ended
up as a member of this group tonight

II how I got there

Sunday afternoons I went to blues jam sessions at the 1369
Club, one of the few places in Boston where both black and
white musicians showed up in about equal numbers. Troy
Starr, a singer who billed himself as "James Brown, Junior,"
asked me to play a job with him and the FBI Band (that's
Funk Busters International).

Rehearsal was the following Sunday at Butch the producer's
house in Mission Hill, where the basement was a private
club with bar and bandstand. Darrell was the drummer in
the FBI Band and Lee was the bass player. I remember Dar-
rell struck me as very serious, and I remember Lee made a
point of coming over to introduce himself to me.

After rehearsal Darrell asked me if I wanted to come with
him and Lee to meet a singing group, the Perfect Blend, for
whom he was putting together a new backup band, and I
went, to another basement, which was not a club but the
dirty cellar of a very dilapidated tenement. Then, when I
unpacked my sax, and Darrell and Lee and Tom and Ken-
roth started to play, and the Blend stood there together and
began to sing "My Girl," I felt like this was something I had
been waiting a long time for.

III my adjustment

I brought things to our basement rehearsal
space sometimes as if I was moving in
to my first apartment   excited that

now we'd have a broom to keep the worst of
the dirt under control   an old lamp for
the back corner where I parked my music
stand next to Lee's bass amp   I brought extension
cords   old tables   brighter light bulbs: one night

miraculously in the crumbling cement
wall I uncovered a phone jack   the next
Sunday I brought my office desk phone and
triumphant plugged it in—my adjustment

was complete: maybe I did have to step
carefully through the doorway to the back
room   avoid the hole in the floor six feet
down to the foundation and walk behind
the furnace to piss   but now we had the
Perfect Blend Telephone   and we used it

somebody was always late   I'd call—EJ
had overslept   Garrison was on his way
sometimes at the end of a rehearsal
just before packing up I'd call home
"do you want me to pick up anything?"

as if I was about to hop on the
commuter train to Wellesley instead of
driving to Somerville through the blasted
streets and broken glass at the heart of Roxbury

IV   ethnography lecture

when visiting another culture you
carry with you the complete set of types
you have learned from your own but while there you

must use them sparingly—like pass keys—then
put them back in your pocket   so you have
both hands free to grasp whatever can be
found: it's trying to hold firm to your types
that will squeeze them into stereotypes

my pass key presented me with Garrison
as the charismatic hero   young prince
lady's man   in my wife's video of
the Blend on stage her camera keeps wandering
onto Garrison   we laugh about this

yes she has a high school crush on him   he's
the hero not as leader but as soloist
not the great ruler but the knight-errant

It's Charles who is the wise king   patient   kind
his dignity shines right out   he leads by
moral authority   Charles doesn't shout but
gives counsel   he is never Charlie or Chuck

when we call him "Doc" it's because his last
name is "Doctor":   sometimes on stage we do
that old joke "they call this man the Doctor
because he makes you feel so good"

Kenny is the eternal hero's friend
Panza   the innocent straight man   the faithful
if someone's feet get tangled on stage it
will be Kenny   he misses the bus to
rehearsal but who can be angry: the
sweetness of his holy disposition
surpasses all of our understanding

and EJ is the outlaw   short-tempered
and proud   his life outside the group is the
most shadowy   he lives in the projects
he changes jobs   his car crashes mysteriously

he has a wife and seven children   no
one speaks about EJ's problems: we
sense him rising above their surface to
be with us: his great gift is loyalty

V   the history of the Perfect Blend

Charles, EJ, Kenny, and Lucky began singing together as a group about 1975. They used various backup bands, generated a small following locally, had a casual brush with at least one Boston record producer, though nothing came of it. They all stayed in their day jobs—clerical or maintenance work in hospitals, banks, insurance companies—and the group was always part-time.

In 1985, Garrison replaced Lucky; Tom (a friend of Charles from work) and Darrell joined the backup band, then the rest of us. Over a two-year period, we played maybe twenty gigs: not enough to build and maintain momentum. The two or three evenings at the Sky Cap were high points. The sense of inertia and the bickering were low points. Garrison, always the most ambitious, said he was quitting. He stayed, though, on a job-to-job basis, neither in nor out.

Finally a woman singer Charles had found was to join the group—she came to one Sky Cap gig to watch, and we were all introduced. Then, somehow, she *was* the group; the rest of the singers had quit. I never knew quite how this happened. Only the name was left: ultimately new singers and a new band got added.

Charles gave up singing to concentrate on electrician courses where he worked, so he could move up from the maintenance yard crew. Kenny I lost track of. Garrison turned up singing in a five-person "Motown Revue," with pre-taped musical arrangements, his moves and his voice as beautiful as always; but they were using him mostly as a backup singer. EJ suddenly left town to stay with his sister in Seattle—some kind of "trouble," unspoken as always.

Sometimes I run into Lee or Tom at jam sessions; I still love
to be on stage playing with Lee next to me, solid, serious,
rocking. You can do that sometimes with instruments—
come back together, even play the same tunes, glimpse a
feeling you've had before; but it's different with singers.
What four particular voices were like at a particular time
and place cannot be recovered. The group is gone, the
singers scattered, there's no more Perfect Blend.

VI   playlist

"Mercy Mercy Mercy" as an instrumental
to warm up the crowd before the singers
Garrison's high tenor on "The Way You
Do the Things You Do"   Charles looking at his
sweetheart in the audience   his open
smile   singing "My Girl"   and last in the Temps medley
"Treat Her Like a Lady"   with the most
elaborate of all the dance routines   those shiny
shoes flashing   the crowd shouting   proud   excited

Sonji—our frequent guest singer   sister
of Charles' fiancee and of our keyboard
player—her piercing intense duets with
Charles   "You Can't Hurt Me Anymore Baby"
FJ's one big solo is "Stand By Me"

the playlist evolves from the singers' sense of
themselves—clear though unspoken—as part of
the Cholly Atkins/Motown tradition
and from what they hear on the radio

Lisa Lisa   Simply Red   Four Tops   Aretha
Dire Straits   even "Earth Angel" turns up at my
suggestion   to the Blend it is a lush
production New Edition cover   to me
it is my high school days   the Penguins' big hit
and I'm featured along with Garrison
this group can make nearly anything their own

when they all show up at my fiftieth
birthday party I'm very happy   when
they sing their a cappella version of
the Everly Brothers' "Dream" for me I'm
struck with the idea that the Perfect Blend
seems sometimes to be containing the world

VII   song in praise

when I phoned Lee one night he was staying
with a cousin   "Lefred" she called   "it's for you"
so I knew his secret name and I knew
he had lived in Florida and I knew
he had toured once with the old comic Pigmeat
Markham and I knew from his accent he
must have been born someplace in the Caribbean

so much for evidence and conclusion
the rest was all marvel and miracle
you stood on stage next to Lee and you felt
a presence   six feet tall   barrel chest   bass guitar
lightly in his hand   this was the root of
the band's sound   the rock we built our church on

like bass players from time immemorial
Lee's wish was to create the sound of a
band   to have it grow out of his fingers
while he stood as still as possible way
at the back of the stage: when Lee smiled I felt good

who came to greet me   a stranger   as soon
as I walked into that first rehearsal?
who radiated peace like a holy
messenger   the steady one   the center?
who held us all in his hands every time
we played   and rocked us gently as babies?
sweet soul   sweet soul   sweet soul   Lee the bass player

VIII   Perfect Blend jokes

Perfect Blend jokes: one night at the Sky Cap
I'm playing a solo   my sax mike on
a long cord   walking between the tables
a man greets me "have I met you somewhere?"
his friend says to him "no Jim don't you know
they all look alike to us" we all laugh

big wedding party for James Brown Junior
(Troy Starr) and we're all invited to come
bring our instruments   I'm on stage jamming
my wife is in back watching   two women
walk by   see her   see me on stage   conclude
we're together   one woman says to her
"I know what you're waiting for   you're waiting
for him to get his black ass down here and go home"

summer gig in the park   I'm introducing
"Earth Angel"   "I'd like to say that all through
high school I performed this song together
with my family and it had special
meaning for us   so tonight I'd like to
do this song the way we used to with—
here he is—my twin brother Garrison!"

the best Perfect Blend joke is the one I
didn't make though I really wanted to:
rehearsal before our gig at the Parker
Street Lounge   a club across the street from the
Mission Hill Projects where EJ lives

it's supposed to be a dangerous place
EJ says it's his neighborhood and there's
nothing to worry about   he'll be looking
out for   taking care of   the white guys in the band

and I want to make this joke but I feel
since I cannot imagine it into
truth   would not wish it into fact   I can't
make it   "EJ" I wish I could say   "EJ
there's no white guys in this band"

middle age

I remember middle age now that you
mention it   that stage I went through in
high school   you can see it in the photos:
seventeen-year-old about to become
oldest Eagle Scout in history as
he receives his badge from the officials

it's clear from the look on his face that he
knows those in authority are pleased   yet
the suspicion is there too   faintly   as
if it's just struck him   that all of this shit
he's been through might really not have been worth it
is it possible he has been conned here?

but the next picture shows development
from this resignation to a quite active
acceptance: on the yearbook page featuring
the heads of National Honor Society
members   here I am   solemn as the proverbial
owl   hair cut short as if I really might

believe that my brain needed room to expand
here I am staring out at you from my
middle age as if to assure you that
my intelligence is now on duty

that the weight of all the world's decisions
can safely rest on me and the others
of my class   so that all of you with less
competence in really complex matters
can just relax and let us handle things

and if you look very closely into
those eyes you see that again something has
just struck me   this time it's the conviction

that since I've suffered and struggled to cope
with this awesome responsibility
which is after all mostly for your benefit
then it's only right that you should pay for it

this was so long ago   my middle age
that I had almost forgotten it
you can see why   it was a scary and
disgusting experience   and as you can
imagine I am happy to have outlived it

all aboard

just a few months short of turning sixty
I'm waiting for my departure toward
old age   patient but anxious   don't know how
fast a trip it will be: I'm so hot for

sex that I could spend years as a horny
old goat   wilting slowly   or instead just
wake up one day and find that the express
has left the station   gone   and will I be

like my father   who chugs merrily on
engine strong though memory   removing
its conductor's cap   has sat down in the
last car to gaze calmly out the window

or will it be quick: I'm on stage playing the sax
"Night Train" and suddenly there's the tunnel ahead

Ghost Radio

fable

I

"if I could only find a white man" said
Sam Phillips (to his associate Marion
Keisker so the story goes   sitting around his
Sun Record offices in Memphis   say 1952)
"who had the Negro sound and the Negro
feel   I could make a million dollars"   or

maybe he said a billion   joking but not joking
since it did come true   over and over:
white men who could sing like black men   or almost
white women like black women   Elvis only
the first and pretty good at it   while others
though not so good at it   made their millions too

but that's a different story   right then
in the midst of the 1950s Sam
Phillips   dropping all his black artists (so
the story goes)   and riding that first wave of
rockabilly   must have done nearly as
well as he had hoped

II

"This story   short and to the point   might frame"
it says in my notes   "the rest and just by
itself tells a lot"

but I can't quite stop there   or if someone
in my brain had switched on a radio
I can't find and so must listen to   playing
over and over: Big Mama Thornton
and Arthur Big Boy Crudup   ghost
radio of rhythm and blues   of joy   pain
pride   anger   that I can't seem to get away from

elegy

John Gill, 1924-1995

he knew me immediately: as a
boy of 14 sees the infant they've just
brought home and says oh my brother's here
before the baby can even tell him-
self from his surroundings

John was that much older   37
both of us teaching at a small college
me the new arrival—hello I
might have said   I have a master's degree
and maybe I'll teach here for my whole life

Come on   he would have said   I still hear his
voice   don't be silly   you're a poet   you
don't fit here any more than I do   he
was sure: even as I'd be thinking which tie
to wear   do I need a haircut   he kept

behaving like both of us were headed
elsewhere   after a while I was sure too
and he was right   now like a kid I have

this urge to talk with him and he's gone
off again   John when you went were you as
I knew you: calm   funny   serene   wicked
tender?   well   brother John was here but he's left me

two sonnets on the death of Richard Nixon

1

"now Hitler " they said "Hitler's foreign
policy was yes seriously flawed
even disastrous   and his treatment of
the Jews   the Gypsies   the queers   the others
was certainly controversial but as
for his domestic policy let's not
forget that he made the German people
for quite some time feel good about themselves"

and as his Secretary of State said
at the funeral he shaped the course of
the world and as others said he was a
towering intellect   he never gave
up   and as Billy Graham said we will
meet him again in heaven when we die

2

I always knew who Richard Nixon was
and he never knew who I was: suppose
it were the other way around   he knew
me and then I died   what would he say   "let
me say this about that"   he'd say   "this man
started as a Communist dupe or worse
expressed his lack of patriotism
during the war in Vietnam   didn't
stop being a radical till he died"

short shrift is what I would get from Nixon
and I'll give the same: war criminal   cheap
crook   sleaze master   weasel scumbag of politics
funeral speeches could not erase this:
Nixon's place in history is assured

remembering Roy Orbison
(December, 1988)

"You turned around/ and walked away/ with me."

I

Later the same day an informal talk
has been scheduled in a small room at the University
where Linda our next door neighbor and I both work

I had seen the modest leaflet a week
before   posted near the elevator
"Rhythm and Jews" it said "Rhythm and Jews:
The Influence of Jews on Early Rock and Roll"
the crowd this attracts is about as large
as you'd expect—Linda   me   maybe six others

the speaker   a young man perhaps thirty
says that if you look at the emergence
of rock and roll from the early fifties on
you see that some of the people in it were Jewish—
this appears to be all that he has to say
I smile as it strikes me that putting the
topic the other way round would be
more interesting: "The Influence of
Early Rock and Roll on Jews"   Linda and I
look at each other and I wonder
if she has had the same thought

II

After the talk we stay for cookies and
juice   Linda raises her cup saying "we
should have a moment for Roy   who died
last night"   "you know" I say   "it's funny   right
after I heard the news at home on the

radio first thing this morning I felt
like I could hear your voice   Linda   singing
'Running Scared'   she laughs   everyone else looks
puzzled and slightly embarrassed until
we explain our little joke: "neighbors   houses
with a common wall   very easy to
hear each other singing in the shower"

then they laugh too although of course only
Linda and I can really share such moments
hearing somebody's music over and over
tapping out messages   knocking on that
wall at dawn sometimes   unseen intimacy of neighbors

"did you hear anything different" she says
"well   I thought I heard two voices" I say
"sounded like you and Julie both singing"
"that's right" Linda says "and at the end we
      hit the high note"

gloss on "Me and Bobby McGee"

twenty years after I met you ten years
since I've seen you and I wake up one day
with Janis Joplin singing in my head
"Me and Bobby McGee" *Bobby shared the*

secrets of my soul she sings and *through all
kinds of weather Bobby baby kept me
from the cold world* nothing like this happened
between us no secrets and no comfort

after so long your face is not clear in
my mind but your voice is as present as
Janis' voice why is that *freedom's just
another word for nothing left to lose*

I was always free to give up my long
obsession with you but I chose not to
I guess I still had something left to lose

*one day I missed Salinas I let him
slip away he was looking for that home
and I hope he finds it* I have found it

but I didn't slip away I was cool
we wished each other well and I left town
not like a singer but a listener—
now every few years Janis turns up this way
just for a couple of days and then she's gone

saxophone

for Adolphe Sax, 1814-1894

in Adolphe Sax's Paris atelier
around 1855   his men are cutting
pounding on sheets of metal as Sax himself
walks up and down the row of workbenches

checking measurements   or the curve of this piece
as it gets hammered into a bell   or
he's testing the seal where this little disc
of cork has to fit airtight against the
small neat hole in the brass tube

it's the heyday of military bands
in Second Empire France where Sax has become
a huge success: flamboyant genius   inventor
artisan from small-town Belgium   he has beat out all
the competition in the great contests
with his "Saxhorns"   an entire family
of brasses in every orchestral range
from highest to lowest   loud   smooth   and flashy

and Berlioz   among others   has praised
Sax's version of the bass clarinet
as much superior to the older ones

but this latest work   weird hybrid of reeds
and brasses that can sing or growl   dancing
while the others march   this is the golden
child that will survive him   triumphant and shining

for Sax himself goes on to establish
a saxophone class at the Conservatory
and though he soon falls into political
disfavor and dies long-lived but poor
it's only ten years until the birth of Coleman Hawkins

Grand Tour 1963

My first trip to Europe the ship docked
in Ireland   I was twenty-five   which in
those days was either younger or older
than it is now—I forget which—seeing

a Dublin phone book I wondered if Yeats
was listed   or rather Mrs. Yeats   who
as far as I knew was still alive: ah! Yeats
Georgie   I could take a cab to her house

an old woman answers the door   "Mrs.
Yeats?"   "yes   are you the doctor?"   "no I just
wanted to tell you how much I like your
husband's poetry"   "thank you"   from Dublin

on to London then Paris   I always had
my trumpet with me   though I was rusty
barely fumbling my way through what we used to call
"Dixieland"   but finding myself one night

at "le Chat Qui Peche" jazz club I asked Chet
Baker if I could sit in   he gave me
that cold stare   a nod   "Ray's Idea" he says
and takes off at an impossible speed

I squeaked a few notes and then just stood there
until—abruptly—they ended the set
another day I phoned Man Ray   "I am
your cousin Elsie's grandson"   we had lunch

chatted at his studio—a nice man
but I knew little at that time about
his work so didn't get much out of it
and didn't go back to see him again

then one night I was watching the TV
news at dinner with a French family
just as Kennedy was shot in Dallas:
we saw the car   the shot   the panic   but

when the news flash said "le President est
blessé" I didn't know enough French so
I thought they were saying that he'd been blessed

portrait in rhythm and blues

I

former National Republican Party Chairman
Lee Atwater had many opportunities
to integrate his love for black music
with his career in politics   for example
when he was Bush's campaign manager

it was his feeling for those people and
their music that suggested to him how
the photo of a black man's face could be
used to influence what white voters did

likewise the sweet soul music featured at
Inauguration festivities: few
other strategists would have understood

how to offset any previous
damage by framing an appeal to the
older middle-class blacks not as blacks but
as fellow members of the middle class

and then a master stroke: the Chairman of
the Republican Party as Howard
University Trustee   in my mind's

eye Lee Atwater pulls up in a pink
Cadillac for his first Board meeting   rings
flash on his hands   he's in a gold-sequined
suit   a sharp valet carries his guitar
"Dig it brothers" he says "I'm your soul man"

but it didn't work out   some students claimed
he didn't respect them or their music:
they doubted his sincerity so much
that he was forced to retire from the Board
disappointed and with his feelings hurt

100

II

then Lee Atwater died of brain cancer
so if I wasn't respectful of the dead
I'd make some joke about how his thinking
had been sick for a long time anyway
and so forth   but I won't do that   instead

I'll give him credit for his letters of
regret to Dukakis and others though
he still didn't repudiate the man
his slimebucket cleverness helped elect

my naturally generous nature
will let that pass   I'll even credit him
with really liking the music   which makes
his betrayal of it all the more un-
forgivable   and I know that if there
are private hells for those who deserve them

there's a special one for Lee Atwater:
they've given him an office but there are
no phones   no campaign to run   no one to
manipulate   there are no Inaugural
Balls where soul music can be made to lick
the Presidential shoes   instead through all
eternity Lee Atwater sits behind
a big desk listening to *Pat Boone's Greatest Hits*

friendship

Ron and Gary have AIDS   Gary will die
first   maybe next week but Ron   my wife's old
friend from the innocent 70s is
healthier   he's nursing Gary at home

while I'm in San Francisco I visit:
Gary is blind now from the lymphoma
and sleeps while I'm there   Ron looks thin   older

I think about the day we met Gary
he was shy   guarded   not sure he could trust
me and Abby   the four of us driving
from Boston to rural New Hampshire for
Ron's father's funeral   stopping at a
restaurant for dinner Gary's concerned:

how will Ron's French-Canadian family
respond to him   and the friends   neighbors
how should he behave   and be introduced

"that's easy" I say "you wear a great big
badge that says *Hi! I'm Ron's lover Gary*"
we all laughed at that and then became friends
so good-bye Gary   here's a kiss on the cheek

seven answers chosen at random to the same question

why do you keep writing political poems?
for twenty-five years my refrigerator
has just seemed to acquire things: milk eggs
tomatoes beef carrots cheese pie lettuce
bacon bread celery cream oranges
until now it will not hold anymore

why do you keep writing political poems?
something got stuck in my throat: I think it's
Vietnam: millions of tiny little bones

why do you keep writing political poems?
as the newspaper recently noted:
"last night a woman was raped   however
it has been speculated that she may
have provoked the alleged rape by something
in her behavior or the way she was dressed"

why do you keep writing political poems?
same newspaper   "FAGS MURDERED: however
it has been speculated that they may
have provoked the alleged murder by
something in their behavior or the way they were dressed"

why do you keep writing political poems?
after Wounded Knee in 1890
I forgot   until Wounded Knee in
1973 and then I forgot
again—please excuse me

why do you keep writing political poems?
last night on my favorite comedy
show the best joke was "Two Polacks"   "Two Spics"
"Two Irish Drunks" "Two Little Japs"   I want
to say how much I respect the great
American gift of laughter

why do you keep writing political poems?
when I try to recall the phone numbers
of old friends   all I can find in my head
is an apparently endless list—under
the heading Black People Who Got Killed Young—
of names I don't recognize   echoing

through me until they start to become vaguely
familiar: Addie Mae Collins   Phillip
Gibbs   James Earl Green   Denise McNair   Carol
Robertson   Cynthia Wesley   and more
they seem to go on and on

four letters to the dead

John Gill

the box arrives by mail: not your ashes
but your last poems   journals   the secrets
you wanted to keep—as writers do—by
putting them on paper   and someone must
read it all to compose your final book

why not me? I'm too sad to write one more
poem about your death John as I had
planned—maybe better to poke through the box:
any juicy secrets? some good gossip?

here's a journal   dream fragments   here's a long
elegy to break the heart that you wrote
last year when your son was killed in a crash
at 33 and here is a page where
just in passing you wrote down my name so

why not me to do this job dear old friend—
as for my own poem all I really need
is a line or two   maybe what you said
to me on the phone from the hospital
"well Dick we had some good times didn't we?"

Cynthia Lasky

as if you were still alive I find I'm
writing to you   Cynthia   friend of my
own generation   my exact age   dead
a week now of cancer   that long disease

and no one who reads these words will be you
that "you" I kissed and talked with now is ashes
and what is my exhausted sadness except:

the weight of all we had still to talk about
the pages—thousands—you never got to write
and the smell of that strong coffee—cups and cups—
that you and I would have drunk together

Carol Baum

it's my first visit to Martha's Vineyard
in eight years   the last time I came it was
to see you one more time before you died
here in the hospital of cancer at 38

I'm thinking how present sometimes you seem
to me   not like a ghost but a witness
to things I know you would have laughed about
that didn't happen till after your death

like the way my music has changed since the days
when our group of friends would sit around with
only my clunky guitar-playing to
help us sing those Carter Family songs
hymns   Woody Guthrie   "Amazing Grace"

106

you sang too   because you loved us   your old
left folky friends   but really   at heart   you
were always a rock and roller: and just

lately I've realized how much it was
rock and roll which nourished in your soul
the brilliant irreverence that we loved

tonight I am wishing you'd been alive
to see me take saxophone lessons and
join an "All-Fifties Rock 'n' Roll Band"

now arrived with our Hawaiian shirts to play
for a wedding party in stuffy old
Edgartown   not five miles from where you died

and I'm not surprised that it's you I think of
when we open all the windows to blast out
something from when you were fourteen years old:

this absurd tune with the Mexican name
and the pseudo-Latin beat   now the band
kicks up   and I blow loud   louder until
I fall down on the church floor still playing
kicking my legs up   pretending to be
mad   ecstatic   carried off by music

and with my eyes closed I look hard for you
your long dark hair   your red dress   the glass of
Coca-Cola in your hand as always:
joyful and raucous   laughing you join in
as we end with a crash and shout "Tequila!"

Gloria Lourie Scheiner

Gloria   master of the long farewell
of the phone conversation without end
of being late as a point of honor
how could we know that you would leave so fast

wasn't that you at family events
life of the party just by putting on
your coat for hours as you made sure not to
miss anyone   stopping for goodbyes
and news from each person you happened to
love between the living room and front door

the party swirled around you   in your coat
you were in your element   most at home
as if being on your way made you joyous
attentive   a natural traveler—
being late then   or slow   was only
another aspect of the grand journey

and wasn't that you   young   Brooklyn College
when one of your brothers wrote to another
what we do is at ten minutes to nine
we hold the front door open and just hope
that Gloria makes it to class on time

it was you   I am sure   who spent more than
fifty years in my life   never hurrying
Aunt Gloria   always Gloria   just
thirteen when I was born   who loved me as
an infant and never stopped   whose final
words to me were "my eldest nephew"

and now Gloria   you want us just to
say our farewells   just like that   not a moment to
put our coats on   take a long look at you
tell you our news   all right   you can go now
but at the next party I'll think of you swirling
toward the door   conversation without end

Indian suicide rates

for Sherman

scholars could spend years debating this one:
if the Indians had won all the wars
after say 1800 would they have
stuck me on a reservation   would some
smart-assed Indian have provided me
with a buffalo robe full of smallpox

would the Indians now excel in pro-
fessional sports and be calling their teams
the Cleveland Polacks   the California
Wops   the New York Micks   the Dakota Jews

would it then be me the experts were looking
at   and my sisters and brothers there on
the reservation or in the shit-hole
end of the city with all the other
losers   watching TV Westerns until
that new movie comes out   what was it called—
"Dances With White Folks?"

and if it was us the experts watched survive
or fall apart   would that bring them any
closer then to asking some of the real
questions like: in whose interest is it
that all these deaths have come to be called suicide?

the real Mount Rushmore

Columbus Day, 1991: for Peter Scheiner and
Andrai Pawlak-Whitted

there's a small mural depicting the real
Mount Rushmore on the wall of a blues club
called Buddy Guy's Legends at the corner
of State and Wabash Streets in Chicago

which as you probably know is the real
city of the blues   furthermore Buddy
Guy is a real blues man and so I thought
this is the right place to look for true national
symbols and real American history

for example a Sunday night blues jam
black white Indian Hispanic Asian
musicians and audience   and speaking
of Columbus two guys from Italy
their English not great but their blues fluent

TC and the Bluejays are the house band
after their set TC starts calling the
jammers one or two at a time on stage
introducing them like guests of honor—
some of them in fact are famous   others
will never be   it's all blues all the time

Lefty Diz was there in a sharp suit and
tie   hat   he grabbed a guitar   played high notes
no one had ever heard   up past the last fret
played one hand on guitar one in the air

the Blues Lone Ranger was there singing: a hip-
shaking papa in pale blue shirt and pants
black mask   red bandana   white hat and twin
revolvers on silver-studded gun belt—such
brilliant deconstruction of the Old West

Bluejay was there   "this is the man we named
our band after" said TC "so you know how
we feel about him"   and LB Blues was
there   "this man" said TC "this man lives the blues"

but you wanted to know about the real
Mount Rushmore—so pretend you're at the club and
TC on stage is leading us in a
sort of call and response: "whose faces" he asks
"are on the real Mount Rushmore?"   and he points
to the green wall behind the pool tables

"whose African faces and Indian
cheekbones"   *Muddy Waters* we answer   "whose
heroic faces"   *Sonny Boy Williamson*
we shout   "whose sweet saintly faces are chiseled"
Little Walter   Howlin Wolf "into that stone mountain?"

in the Catskills again

my wife's bare footprints on these rocks after
she's been swimming where the river has dug
a small pool by the road outside Bearsville

it looks like rain   no   it's raining   should I
follow these delicate marks to find her
no   she's just ten feet away   and she turns

back   green bathing suit   thin legs   orange and
black towel   it stops raining   her footprints
going away have evaporated

but of course she makes new ones heading toward
me   there are certain moments you stay in
even as they're gone   like wet prints on rock
or the way you cannot forget your dead friends

among the Dworkins

Carol and Denise by coincidence
are both visiting me on the same day:
acquaintances without much in common —
the New York Jewish princess married to
one of my best friends and the great poet
my first teacher who I still feel close to

by chance it's also the day my brother
phones: "let me talk to him"   says Denise in
a playful mood   they've met a few times and
she does have this small streak of mischief   "he'll
never guess it's me"   and sure enough when

she says in her British accent   "do you
know who this is?"   my brother at a loss
casting about   lights on some old friends of
my father — an English couple and their
children: "it sounds" he says   "like a Dworkin"

"he thinks"   Denise reports   her hand over
the phone "it's a Dworkin"   and just the word
itself sends Denise and Carol into
shrieking hysterical fits that somehow

establish a particular close bond
that lasts until Carol's illness and death
eight years later—they exchange "Dear Dworkin"
letters   little elf statues   they greet each
other "hello Dworkin" and are prone at
any time and in public to collapse
giggling   this shared identity suits the
two of them in some mysterious and

deeply comic way   it's the kind of joke
most people greet with polite silence at
best   and of course incomprehension   now

Denise is gone too and   of everything
there is to remember   what I think of
is the way she and Carol came to my
house that day and how they laughed

friends in dreams

I

dead friends enter a dream as if they were
on their way to pay that visit   the one
you had postponed for some not very
important reason and which would have been your
last one with them—who could have known of course   and
they haven't come to blame you: nevertheless
as they walk toward you through the parking lot
(were you supposed to meet them here?) they come
only so far as to be unmistakably
themselves   and then stop—it's not as in your
waking life some person who from a distance
shockingly resembles the dead   no   this is
that face of a friend who (even as the
dream seems real) you know you have called forth from
wherever the dead are

not speaking you both wave   and you wonder:
why here?   what is signified by this place
neat rows of empty cars   no one else around?
and: should you try to speak   to touch   like Odysseus?
your friend will not come close enough for that—
still   waking   you know you have the power
at least to see that face when you need to

II

friends still alive come in always without
knocking and through unexpected doors and
in disguise: some   who were never your lovers
have changed sex   they pursue you gently   those
who had been your lovers before settling

into friendship turn moony and playful
again   they sneak into your house to pinch
your ass in the shower   laughing: they seem
to have forgiven everything   and all
your other friends are liable to show up too   as
if your sleep was the great costume party of the year

one is dressed as your mother and father—
both at once—another turns up as the
assassin you have always feared   your dog
trots in disguised as one of those few teachers
you ever got along with in high school
someone you see every week of your life
is the Invisible Man from H.G. Wells
in a black suit   the face a swath of tape
so as to be seen at all   and that friend
you never see but who you have been meaning to
write to of course arrives as   who else?   you.

                        III

but the friends who you know are dying now   these
will call on you differently in sleep:
for one thing you have learned by now to think
of every visit as the last   you are careful to
speak   to touch   while you still can   and you study
that face of a friend you love so you could
never mistake it for anyone else's

disguise is equally impossible—
in these faces what they have been their whole
lives   or could have been   or wanted to be
is finally there for you to see   all
at once   so that if   now or afterward
they do visit your dreams   walk into your
house   the costume party will vanish like

a fairy tale as your dying friends grasp your
hands in their strong hands   look in your eyes and
lead you in a dance of life.